Get Outside
BE AN ANIMAL TRACKER

EMILY KINGTON

HUNGRY TOMATO™

CONTENTS

BE AN ANIMAL TRACKER

HELPFUL TOOLS
- Gloves
- Rain boots
- Old bag to carry items home
- Small trowel or old spoon
- Scissors

Going outside is lots of fun, and we can get crafty at the same time. You'll learn how to help animals and make fun projects from things you can find outside.

Get your rain boots on and go on a scavenger hunt. Turn the page to see what things you'll need to find . . .

You will need a grown-up to help make these fun nature projects.

SCAVENGER HUNT

You need to find...

Moss

Dig it up from the forest floor. It's best if it has a little dirt.

Leaves

Find dry leaves of all shapes and sizes.

Vines

Vine stems can be used to tie things together.

Sticks

Always be on the lookout for sticks of all different sizes.

Stones and Pebbles

Look for different shapes, sizes, and colors.

Dry Grass

Birds use grass to make their nests.

Pine cones

Pine cones will help make your projects look great!

Logs

Animals hide under logs to stay dry when it's raining.

YOU WILL ALSO NEED

Paper
Super glue
Acrylic paint
Marker
String
Empty water bottle
Orange
Paper cups
Saucepan
Bird food (see page 11)
Paper clay
Cookie cutters
Parchment paper
Bricks
Piece of wood
Paintbrush

LEAF ART

Bring the outside in!

YOU WILL NEED
Four sticks of equal length
Vine stems
Small leaves of different
    shapes and sizes
Paintbrush
Paper
Super glue
Acrylic paint
String

1 Brush the sticks
with the paintbrush to clean them.
Take the leaves off a few vine stems..

2 Glue the sticks
together to
make a square.

Tie the corners
with string to
make them
stronger.

Glue vine stems
across the
square.

3 Tear paper
into pieces.

6

2 Stick the leaves onto the paper. Try to make animal shapes by putting two leaves together, then paint them.

Glue them to the vines to show off your art!

HANGING NESTING BOTTLE

Help birds find the things they need to build their nests.

YOU WILL NEED

Dry grass
Moss
Small sticks
Empty water bottle
Marker
Scissors
Wooden skewer

1 Remove the bottom of the bottle using a pair of scissors.

Ask a grown-up to make holes in the bottle with a wooden skewer and push some small sticks through the holes.

Draw some windows onto the bottle above the sticks.

2 Cut out the windows with scissors.

Fill with dry grass and moss.

3 Add string to the top of the bottle to hang it.

BIRD FEEDERS

Invite birds to your yard with these yummy feeders!

EASY BIRD FEEDER

Birds will love this, and you get to eat the leftover orange!

1 Remove the top and scoop out the inside of a large orange.

Ask a grown-up to make a hole on either side of the orange with a wooden skewer.

2 Push a small twig through the holes.

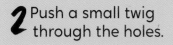

3 Tie both ends of a piece of string around the stick on the outside of the orange.

Fill the orange with bird food. You can buy bird seed from a pet store or use raisins, oats, and nuts.

It will be so fun to watch the birds!

COLD WINTER RECIPE

This feeder can only be made when it's really cold outside. Ask a grown-up if it's cold enough before getting started.

YOU WILL NEED

Paper cups
String
Saucepan
Wooden skewer
One part lard and two parts raisins, nuts, and oats
Scissors

1 Put the raisins, nuts, and oats in a large bowl.

Ask a grown-up to help you melt the lard in a saucepan.

Take it off the heat, then leave to cool a little before pouring in the other ingredients.

2 Have a grown-up help make a hole in the bottom of a paper cup with a wooden skewer.

Put a piece of string through the hole and tie a knot at the bottom.

3 Push the mixture into the cup and around the piece of string.

4 Put in the fridge overnight. Cut open the cup.

5 Hang the feeder outside.

Don't forget to leave some water out for them too!

CREATURE CHECKLIST

Here is a list of animals you can try to find.

SAFETY!

Do not get close to wild animals or insects. They can be dangerous!

1 Bird

You will see lots of birds if you have made the bird feeders.

2 Rabbit

Rabbits live together in groups in underground homes called warrens.

 3 Fox

Foxes live around the world.

14

4 Deer

Deer live in the woods. They look for food during the day.

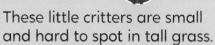

5 Field mouse

These little critters are small and hard to spot in tall grass.

6 Otter

Otters sleep during the day and come out at night.

7 Squirrel

If you hear noises in a tree above you, look up!

8 Frog

Frogs live near streams, lakes, and ponds.

BE AN ANIMAL TRACKER

We may not always see animals on our travels, but what they leave behind tells us they were there.

Cow

POOP!

Look, but don't touch! Every animal's poop is different. It can tell you who is living nearby!

Deer

Rabbit

Bear

Horse

ANIMAL TRACKS

When the ground is soft, look for the tracks that animals have left behind.

Deer

Bear

Dog

Bird

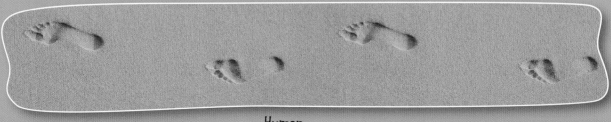

Human

MOLEHILLS

Moles dig tunnels underground. They make molehills when they move dirt out of their tunnels.

SQUIRREL STUFF

Squirrels bury acorns and nuts underground and dig them up in winter when food is hard to find.

BURROWS

Rabbits can dig underground homes that are hundreds of feet long!

BIRD NESTS

Birds lay eggs in nests in the springtime.

NATURAL WIND ART

Use things you found outside
to make this fun art project!

1 Cross two sticks and tie them together with string.

Tie a long piece of string to the end of each stick.

2 Roll out some paper clay and cut out shapes with cookie cutters. Decorate with small stones.

Ask a grown-up to help you make holes in the clay shapes with a wooden skewer.

Leave to dry.

3 Pull string through the paper clay shapes.

4 Tie string around pine cones and leaves.

5 Tie your pine cones, leaves, and paper clay to the sticks.

6 Take the string at the ends of the sticks and tie them together.

Hang it in a gentle breeze!

21

SMALL CRITTER HOME

Build little wood homes for forest animals.

YOU WILL NEED

Two bricks
Piece of wood
Small logs
Small sticks
Dry grass
Dry leaves

1 Find a quiet spot under a tree.

2 Lay down the bricks and small logs.

3 Lay down some dry grass and leaves.

4 Cover with a piece of wood.

5 Put small sticks and leaves on top to hide it.

Now little animals will have a dry place to sleep!

BE CAREFUL OUTSIDE

It's always fun to play outside, but it's a good idea to . . .

. . . take water with you

. . . take a first aid kit for scratches and bug bites

. . . wear clothes and shoes for playing in the woods

. . . tell a grown-up where you are going

Safety First

Don't eat plants, and don't drink water you didn't bring with you.

If you are climbing, make sure you are with a grown-up.

Stay away from wild animals. They could be dangerous!

Be careful near water. It can be deeper than it looks.

Hungry Tomato®
An imprint of Lerner Publishing Group, Inc.
241 First Avenue North
Minneapolis, MN 55401 USA

For reading levels and more information, look up this title at www.lernerbooks.com.

Main body text set in Crossten.

Library of Congress Cataloging-in-Publication Data

Names: Kington, Emily, 1961– author.
Title: Be an animal tracker / Emily Kington.
Description: Minneapolis : Hungry Tomato, [2019] | Series: Get outside! | Audience: Age 6–9. | Audience: Grades K to 3.
Identifiers: LCCN 2019012417 (print) | LCCN 2019014075 (ebook) | ISBN 9781541555228 (eb pdf) | ISBN 9781541555211 (lb : alk. paper)
Subjects: LCSH: Animal tracks–Juvenile literature. | Handicraft–Juvenile literature.
Classification: LCC QL768 (ebook) | LCC QL768 .K56 2019 (print) | DDC 591.47/9–dc23

LC record available at https://lccn.loc.gov/2019012417

Manufactured in the United States of America
1-45928-42822-4/12/2019

PICTURE CREDITS

(abbreviations: t = top; b = bottom; m = middle; l = left; r = right; bg = background)

Shutterstock: A_Lesik 19bl; Ademortuus 14ml; Anton Starikov 5b; binik 17bl; Chris Brannon 18tl; Dmitry Pichugin 18tr; Elena Barenbaum all vector birds; Eric Isselee 14mr, 15tl, ml, mr & br, 24mr & br; fotohunter 19br; FotoRequest 14tr; Hanet all vector animals; Joyce Vincent 24b (bottle); KanphotoSS 17tl; Kozlik 18b; MR.PRAWET THADTHIAM 16tr; photomaster 15tr; prattaph 16bl; Robert Hoetink 18mr; tchara 19tl; Viktor Loki 17mr; WIRACHAIPHOTO 18ml; Zhukov Oleg 14bl.